50 The Art of Soup
Recipes for Home

By: Kelly Johnson

Table of Contents

- Classic Tomato Basil Soup
- Creamy Chicken and Wild Rice Soup
- Butternut Squash Soup with Sage
- Hearty Beef and Barley Soup
- Spicy Black Bean Soup
- Rustic Vegetable Minestrone
- Potato Leek Soup
- Thai Coconut Curry Soup
- French Onion Soup
- Lentil and Vegetable Soup
- Creamy Broccoli Cheddar Soup
- Clam Chowder
- Split Pea Soup with Ham
- Chicken Tortilla Soup
- Mushroom Barley Soup
- Roasted Red Pepper and Tomato Soup
- New England Fish Chowder
- Moroccan Spiced Carrot Soup
- Coconut Lemongrass Soup
- Saffron and Shrimp Soup
- Sweet Potato and Black Bean Soup
- Gazpacho
- Creamy Cauliflower Soup
- Greek Lemon Chicken Soup (Avgolemono)
- Cabbage and Sausage Soup
- Italian Wedding Soup
- Curried Pumpkin Soup
- Egg Drop Soup
- Italian Pepper Soup
- Chilled Avocado Soup
- Beef Pho
- Vegetable and Quinoa Soup
- Chicken and Dumpling Soup
- Spicy Tomato and Chickpea Soup
- Wild Rice and Mushroom Soup
- Roasted Garlic and Cauliflower Soup
- Spinach and Feta Soup
- Zucchini and Basil Soup
- Creamy Celery Soup

- Tomato and Basil Bisque
- Chicken and Corn Chowder
- Carrot and Ginger Soup
- Borscht (Beet Soup)
- Cheesy Cauliflower Chowder
- Southwestern Chicken Soup
- Farro and Vegetable Soup
- Lentil and Ham Soup
- Miso Soup with Tofu
- Curry Lentil Soup
- Creamy Seafood Chowder

Classic Tomato Basil Soup

Ingredients:

- 2 cans (28 oz each) crushed tomatoes
- 1 onion, diced
- 3 cloves garlic, minced
- 1 cup vegetable broth
- 1/2 cup fresh basil leaves, chopped
- 1 teaspoon sugar
- Salt and pepper to taste
- 1/2 cup heavy cream (optional)

Instructions:

1. In a large pot, sauté onion and garlic until soft.
2. Add crushed tomatoes, broth, sugar, salt, and pepper; bring to a simmer.
3. Stir in basil and cook for 10 minutes.
4. For a creamy texture, blend the soup, then stir in heavy cream before serving.

Creamy Chicken and Wild Rice Soup

Ingredients:

- 1 cup cooked chicken, shredded
- 1 cup wild rice, cooked
- 1 onion, diced
- 2 carrots, diced
- 2 celery stalks, diced
- 4 cups chicken broth
- 1 cup heavy cream
- Salt and pepper to taste

Instructions:

1. In a large pot, sauté onion, carrots, and celery until soft.
2. Add chicken broth, cooked chicken, and wild rice; bring to a boil.
3. Reduce heat and stir in heavy cream, salt, and pepper; simmer for 10 minutes.

Butternut Squash Soup with Sage

Ingredients:

- 1 medium butternut squash, peeled and cubed
- 1 onion, diced
- 2 cloves garlic, minced
- 4 cups vegetable broth
- 1 teaspoon dried sage
- Salt and pepper to taste
- 1/2 cup heavy cream (optional)

Instructions:

1. In a large pot, sauté onion and garlic until soft.
2. Add butternut squash, broth, sage, salt, and pepper; bring to a boil.
3. Simmer until squash is tender, about 20 minutes.
4. Blend until smooth, adding cream if desired.

Hearty Beef and Barley Soup

Ingredients:

- 1 pound beef stew meat, cubed
- 1 onion, diced
- 2 carrots, diced
- 2 celery stalks, diced
- 4 cups beef broth
- 1 cup barley
- 1 teaspoon thyme
- Salt and pepper to taste

Instructions:

1. In a large pot, brown the beef over medium heat.
2. Add onion, carrots, and celery; sauté until softened.
3. Add broth, barley, thyme, salt, and pepper; bring to a boil.
4. Reduce heat and simmer for 1 hour, until barley is tender.

Spicy Black Bean Soup

Ingredients:

- 2 cans (15 oz each) black beans, rinsed and drained
- 1 onion, diced
- 2 cloves garlic, minced
- 1 teaspoon cumin
- 1 teaspoon chili powder
- 4 cups vegetable broth
- 1 jalapeño, diced (optional)
- Salt and pepper to taste

Instructions:

1. In a pot, sauté onion and garlic until soft.
2. Add cumin, chili powder, and jalapeño; cook for another minute.
3. Stir in black beans and broth; bring to a boil.
4. Simmer for 20 minutes, then blend for a smoother texture if desired.

Rustic Vegetable Minestrone

Ingredients:

- 1 onion, diced
- 2 carrots, diced
- 2 celery stalks, diced
- 2 cups mixed vegetables (zucchini, green beans, etc.)
- 1 can (14 oz) diced tomatoes
- 4 cups vegetable broth
- 1 cup pasta (small shapes)
- 1 teaspoon Italian seasoning
- Salt and pepper to taste

Instructions:

1. In a large pot, sauté onion, carrots, and celery until soft.
2. Add mixed vegetables, tomatoes, broth, pasta, Italian seasoning, salt, and pepper; bring to a boil.
3. Reduce heat and simmer until pasta is cooked, about 10 minutes.

Potato Leek Soup

Ingredients:

- 3 leeks, cleaned and sliced
- 4 large potatoes, peeled and diced
- 4 cups vegetable broth
- 1 cup heavy cream
- Salt and pepper to taste

Instructions:

1. In a pot, sauté leeks until soft.
2. Add potatoes and broth; bring to a boil.
3. Simmer until potatoes are tender, about 20 minutes.
4. Blend until smooth and stir in cream before serving.

Thai Coconut Curry Soup

Ingredients:

- 1 can (14 oz) coconut milk
- 4 cups vegetable broth
- 2 tablespoons red curry paste
- 1 cup mushrooms, sliced
- 1 cup bell pepper, sliced
- 1 cup snap peas
- 1 tablespoon lime juice
- Fresh cilantro for garnish

Instructions:

1. In a pot, combine coconut milk, broth, and curry paste; bring to a simmer.
2. Add mushrooms, bell pepper, and snap peas; cook for 5-7 minutes until vegetables are tender.
3. Stir in lime juice and garnish with cilantro before serving.

Enjoy these comforting and flavorful soups!

French Onion Soup

Ingredients:

- 4 large onions, thinly sliced
- 4 cups beef broth
- 1 cup white wine
- 2 tablespoons butter
- 1 teaspoon thyme
- Salt and pepper to taste
- Baguette slices
- 1 cup Gruyère cheese, shredded

Instructions:

1. In a large pot, melt butter over medium heat and sauté onions until caramelized, about 30 minutes.
2. Add white wine and thyme; simmer for 5 minutes.
3. Stir in beef broth, salt, and pepper; simmer for 20 minutes.
4. Serve in bowls topped with baguette slices and cheese, then broil until bubbly.

Lentil and Vegetable Soup

Ingredients:

- 1 cup lentils, rinsed
- 1 onion, diced
- 2 carrots, diced
- 2 celery stalks, diced
- 4 cups vegetable broth
- 1 can (14 oz) diced tomatoes
- 1 teaspoon thyme
- Salt and pepper to taste

Instructions:

1. In a pot, sauté onion, carrots, and celery until soft.
2. Add lentils, broth, tomatoes, thyme, salt, and pepper; bring to a boil.
3. Reduce heat and simmer for 30-35 minutes until lentils are tender.

Creamy Broccoli Cheddar Soup

Ingredients:

- 4 cups broccoli florets
- 1 onion, diced
- 2 cups vegetable broth
- 1 cup heavy cream
- 2 cups cheddar cheese, shredded
- Salt and pepper to taste

Instructions:

1. In a pot, sauté onion until soft.
2. Add broccoli and broth; simmer until broccoli is tender, about 10-15 minutes.
3. Blend until smooth, then stir in cream and cheese until melted.

Clam Chowder

Ingredients:

- 4 slices bacon, chopped
- 1 onion, diced
- 2 cups potatoes, diced
- 2 cups clams (canned or fresh)
- 2 cups clam juice
- 1 cup heavy cream
- Salt and pepper to taste

Instructions:

1. In a pot, cook bacon until crispy; remove and set aside.
2. Sauté onion in bacon fat until soft.
3. Add potatoes and clam juice; bring to a boil.
4. Reduce heat, add clams, cream, and season with salt and pepper. Simmer for 10 minutes.

Split Pea Soup with Ham

Ingredients:

- 1 cup split peas, rinsed
- 1 onion, diced
- 2 carrots, diced
- 2 celery stalks, diced
- 4 cups vegetable or chicken broth
- 1 cup diced ham
- Salt and pepper to taste

Instructions:

1. In a pot, sauté onion, carrots, and celery until soft.
2. Add split peas, broth, ham, salt, and pepper; bring to a boil.
3. Reduce heat and simmer for 30-40 minutes until peas are tender.

Chicken Tortilla Soup

Ingredients:

- 2 cups cooked chicken, shredded
- 1 can (14 oz) diced tomatoes
- 1 can (15 oz) black beans, rinsed
- 1 onion, diced
- 4 cups chicken broth
- 1 teaspoon chili powder
- Tortilla strips for serving
- Avocado and cilantro for garnish

Instructions:

1. In a pot, sauté onion until soft.
2. Add tomatoes, black beans, chicken, broth, and chili powder; bring to a boil.
3. Simmer for 20 minutes, then serve topped with tortilla strips, avocado, and cilantro.

Mushroom Barley Soup

Ingredients:

- 1 cup barley, rinsed
- 1 onion, diced
- 2 cups mushrooms, sliced
- 2 carrots, diced
- 4 cups vegetable broth
- 1 teaspoon thyme
- Salt and pepper to taste

Instructions:

1. In a pot, sauté onion and mushrooms until softened.
2. Add carrots, barley, broth, thyme, salt, and pepper; bring to a boil.
3. Reduce heat and simmer for 45-50 minutes until barley is tender.

Roasted Red Pepper and Tomato Soup

Ingredients:

- 2 cans (14 oz each) diced tomatoes
- 2 roasted red peppers, peeled and chopped
- 1 onion, diced
- 3 cloves garlic, minced
- 2 cups vegetable broth
- 1/2 cup heavy cream (optional)
- Salt and pepper to taste

Instructions:

1. In a pot, sauté onion and garlic until soft.
2. Add tomatoes, roasted peppers, and broth; bring to a boil.
3. Simmer for 20 minutes, then blend until smooth. Stir in cream if desired.

Enjoy these comforting soups!

New England Fish Chowder

Ingredients:

- 4 slices bacon, chopped
- 1 onion, diced
- 2 cups potatoes, diced
- 2 cups fish stock
- 2 cups white fish (such as cod), cubed
- 1 cup heavy cream
- Salt and pepper to taste
- Fresh parsley for garnish

Instructions:

1. In a pot, cook bacon until crispy; remove and set aside.
2. Sauté onion in bacon fat until soft.
3. Add potatoes and fish stock; bring to a boil.
4. Reduce heat, add fish, and simmer for 10 minutes.
5. Stir in cream, salt, and pepper; serve garnished with parsley and bacon.

Moroccan Spiced Carrot Soup

Ingredients:

- 1 pound carrots, peeled and chopped
- 1 onion, diced
- 2 cloves garlic, minced
- 1 teaspoon cumin
- 1 teaspoon coriander
- 4 cups vegetable broth
- 1 tablespoon olive oil
- Salt and pepper to taste
- Fresh cilantro for garnish

Instructions:

1. In a pot, heat olive oil and sauté onion and garlic until soft.
2. Add carrots, cumin, and coriander; cook for 5 minutes.
3. Pour in broth and bring to a boil.
4. Simmer until carrots are tender, about 20 minutes.
5. Blend until smooth and season with salt and pepper. Garnish with cilantro.

Coconut Lemongrass Soup

Ingredients:

- 1 can (14 oz) coconut milk
- 4 cups vegetable broth
- 2 stalks lemongrass, chopped
- 1 tablespoon ginger, minced
- 1 cup mushrooms, sliced
- 1 cup baby spinach
- 1 tablespoon lime juice
- Salt to taste

Instructions:

1. In a pot, combine coconut milk, broth, lemongrass, and ginger; bring to a simmer.
2. Add mushrooms and cook for 10 minutes.
3. Stir in spinach and lime juice; season with salt before serving.

Saffron and Shrimp Soup

Ingredients:

- 1 pound shrimp, peeled and deveined
- 1 onion, diced
- 2 cloves garlic, minced
- 1 teaspoon saffron threads
- 4 cups seafood stock
- 1 cup diced tomatoes
- Salt and pepper to taste
- Fresh cilantro for garnish

Instructions:

1. In a pot, sauté onion and garlic until soft.
2. Add saffron, seafood stock, and tomatoes; bring to a boil.
3. Add shrimp and simmer until cooked, about 5 minutes.
4. Season with salt and pepper and garnish with cilantro.

Sweet Potato and Black Bean Soup

Ingredients:

- 2 cups sweet potatoes, diced
- 1 can (15 oz) black beans, rinsed
- 1 onion, diced
- 4 cups vegetable broth
- 1 teaspoon cumin
- 1 teaspoon chili powder
- Salt and pepper to taste

Instructions:

1. In a pot, sauté onion until soft.
2. Add sweet potatoes, black beans, broth, cumin, chili powder, salt, and pepper; bring to a boil.
3. Simmer until sweet potatoes are tender, about 20 minutes. Blend for a smoother texture if desired.

Gazpacho

Ingredients:

- 4 ripe tomatoes, chopped
- 1 cucumber, diced
- 1 bell pepper, diced
- 1 onion, diced
- 3 cups tomato juice
- 2 tablespoons olive oil
- 1 tablespoon red wine vinegar
- Salt and pepper to taste
- Fresh basil for garnish

Instructions:

1. In a blender, combine tomatoes, cucumber, bell pepper, onion, tomato juice, olive oil, vinegar, salt, and pepper.
2. Blend until smooth. Chill in the refrigerator for at least 1 hour before serving.
3. Garnish with fresh basil.

Creamy Cauliflower Soup

Ingredients:

- 1 head cauliflower, chopped
- 1 onion, diced
- 4 cups vegetable broth
- 1 cup heavy cream
- 2 cloves garlic, minced
- Salt and pepper to taste

Instructions:

1. In a pot, sauté onion and garlic until soft.
2. Add cauliflower and broth; bring to a boil.
3. Simmer until cauliflower is tender, about 15 minutes.
4. Blend until smooth, then stir in cream and season with salt and pepper.

Greek Lemon Chicken Soup (Avgolemono)

Ingredients:

- 1 cup cooked chicken, shredded
- 4 cups chicken broth
- 1/2 cup rice
- 2 eggs
- 1/4 cup lemon juice
- Salt and pepper to taste
- Fresh dill for garnish

Instructions:

1. In a pot, bring chicken broth and rice to a boil; simmer until rice is tender.
2. In a bowl, whisk eggs and lemon juice.
3. Gradually add hot broth to the egg mixture to temper it, then stir back into the pot.
4. Add chicken, season with salt and pepper, and garnish with dill before serving.

Enjoy these delicious and comforting soups!

Cabbage and Sausage Soup

Ingredients:

- 1 pound smoked sausage, sliced
- 1 onion, diced
- 2 carrots, diced
- 4 cups cabbage, chopped
- 4 cups vegetable or chicken broth
- 1 can (14 oz) diced tomatoes
- 1 teaspoon thyme
- Salt and pepper to taste

Instructions:

1. In a large pot, sauté sausage until browned; remove and set aside.
2. Sauté onion and carrots until soft.
3. Add cabbage, broth, tomatoes, thyme, salt, and pepper; bring to a boil.
4. Reduce heat, stir in sausage, and simmer for 20-30 minutes.

Italian Wedding Soup

Ingredients:

- 1 pound meatballs (store-bought or homemade)
- 1 onion, diced
- 2 carrots, diced
- 2 celery stalks, diced
- 4 cups chicken broth
- 1 cup small pasta (like acini di pepe)
- 2 cups spinach or kale
- Salt and pepper to taste
- Grated Parmesan for serving

Instructions:

1. In a pot, sauté onion, carrots, and celery until softened.
2. Add broth and bring to a boil; add meatballs and pasta.
3. Simmer until meatballs are cooked and pasta is tender, about 10-12 minutes.
4. Stir in greens, season with salt and pepper, and serve with Parmesan.

Curried Pumpkin Soup

Ingredients:

- 1 can (15 oz) pumpkin puree
- 1 onion, diced
- 2 cloves garlic, minced
- 4 cups vegetable broth
- 1 tablespoon curry powder
- 1 cup coconut milk
- Salt and pepper to taste
- Fresh cilantro for garnish

Instructions:

1. In a pot, sauté onion and garlic until soft.
2. Stir in curry powder and cook for 1 minute.
3. Add pumpkin puree and broth; bring to a simmer.
4. Stir in coconut milk, season with salt and pepper, and blend until smooth. Garnish with cilantro.

Egg Drop Soup

Ingredients:

- 4 cups chicken broth
- 2 eggs, beaten
- 1 tablespoon cornstarch mixed with 2 tablespoons water
- 1 teaspoon ginger, minced
- 2 green onions, sliced
- Salt and pepper to taste

Instructions:

1. In a pot, bring chicken broth and ginger to a boil.
2. Add cornstarch mixture and simmer until slightly thickened.
3. Slowly drizzle in beaten eggs while stirring the broth to create egg ribbons.
4. Season with salt and pepper, and garnish with green onions before serving.

Italian Pepper Soup

Ingredients:

- 1 onion, diced
- 2 bell peppers, diced
- 2 cloves garlic, minced
- 4 cups vegetable or chicken broth
- 1 can (14 oz) diced tomatoes
- 1 teaspoon Italian seasoning
- Salt and pepper to taste

Instructions:

1. In a pot, sauté onion, bell peppers, and garlic until softened.
2. Add broth, tomatoes, Italian seasoning, salt, and pepper; bring to a boil.
3. Reduce heat and simmer for 20 minutes before serving.

Chilled Avocado Soup

Ingredients:

- 2 ripe avocados
- 2 cups vegetable broth
- 1 cup Greek yogurt
- 1 lime, juiced
- 1 clove garlic
- Salt and pepper to taste
- Fresh cilantro for garnish

Instructions:

1. In a blender, combine avocados, broth, yogurt, lime juice, garlic, salt, and pepper.
2. Blend until smooth, then chill in the refrigerator for at least 1 hour.
3. Serve cold, garnished with cilantro.

Beef Pho

Ingredients:

- 1 pound beef (sirloin or brisket), thinly sliced
- 4 cups beef broth
- 1 onion, quartered
- 1 piece ginger, sliced
- 2 star anise
- 1 cinnamon stick
- Rice noodles
- Fresh herbs (basil, cilantro) for garnish
- Lime wedges for serving

Instructions:

1. In a pot, bring beef broth, onion, ginger, star anise, and cinnamon to a boil.
2. Simmer for 30 minutes to infuse flavors.
3. Cook rice noodles according to package instructions.
4. Strain the broth, then serve over noodles with sliced beef, fresh herbs, and lime wedges.

Vegetable and Quinoa Soup

Ingredients:

- 1 cup quinoa, rinsed
- 1 onion, diced
- 2 carrots, diced
- 2 celery stalks, diced
- 4 cups vegetable broth
- 1 can (14 oz) diced tomatoes
- 2 cups mixed vegetables (like green beans, corn)
- Salt and pepper to taste

Instructions:

1. In a pot, sauté onion, carrots, and celery until softened.
2. Add broth, tomatoes, quinoa, mixed vegetables, salt, and pepper; bring to a boil.
3. Reduce heat and simmer for 20 minutes until quinoa is cooked.

Enjoy these hearty and delicious soups!

Chicken and Dumpling Soup

Ingredients:

- 1 pound chicken breast, cooked and shredded
- 1 onion, diced
- 2 carrots, diced
- 2 celery stalks, diced
- 4 cups chicken broth
- 1 teaspoon thyme
- 2 cups biscuit dough (store-bought or homemade)
- Salt and pepper to taste

Instructions:

1. In a pot, sauté onion, carrots, and celery until soft.
2. Add chicken broth, shredded chicken, thyme, salt, and pepper; bring to a simmer.
3. Drop spoonfuls of biscuit dough into the simmering soup.
4. Cover and cook for 15-20 minutes until dumplings are cooked through.

Spicy Tomato and Chickpea Soup

Ingredients:

- 2 cans (14 oz each) diced tomatoes
- 1 can (15 oz) chickpeas, rinsed
- 1 onion, diced
- 2 cloves garlic, minced
- 1 teaspoon cumin
- 1 teaspoon chili powder
- 4 cups vegetable broth
- Salt and pepper to taste

Instructions:

1. In a pot, sauté onion and garlic until soft.
2. Add cumin and chili powder; cook for 1 minute.
3. Stir in tomatoes, chickpeas, broth, salt, and pepper; bring to a boil.
4. Reduce heat and simmer for 20 minutes.

Wild Rice and Mushroom Soup

Ingredients:

- 1 cup wild rice, rinsed
- 1 onion, diced
- 2 cups mushrooms, sliced
- 4 cups vegetable broth
- 2 carrots, diced
- 1 teaspoon thyme
- Salt and pepper to taste

Instructions:

1. In a pot, sauté onion and mushrooms until softened.
2. Add carrots, wild rice, broth, thyme, salt, and pepper; bring to a boil.
3. Reduce heat and simmer for about 45 minutes until rice is tender.

Roasted Garlic and Cauliflower Soup

Ingredients:

- 1 head cauliflower, chopped
- 1 whole head garlic, roasted
- 4 cups vegetable broth
- 1 onion, diced
- 1 cup heavy cream (optional)
- Salt and pepper to taste

Instructions:

1. In a pot, sauté onion until soft.
2. Add cauliflower, roasted garlic, and broth; bring to a boil.
3. Simmer until cauliflower is tender, about 15-20 minutes.
4. Blend until smooth, then stir in cream if desired.

Spinach and Feta Soup

Ingredients:

- 4 cups fresh spinach
- 1 onion, diced
- 4 cups vegetable broth
- 1 cup feta cheese, crumbled
- 1 cup Greek yogurt (optional)
- Salt and pepper to taste

Instructions:

1. In a pot, sauté onion until soft.
2. Add spinach and broth; bring to a simmer.
3. Stir in feta, season with salt and pepper, and blend until smooth.
4. If using, stir in Greek yogurt before serving.

Zucchini and Basil Soup

Ingredients:

- 3 medium zucchinis, chopped
- 1 onion, diced
- 4 cups vegetable broth
- 1 cup fresh basil leaves
- 1 cup heavy cream (optional)
- Salt and pepper to taste

Instructions:

1. In a pot, sauté onion until soft.
2. Add zucchini and broth; bring to a boil.
3. Simmer until zucchini is tender, about 10 minutes.
4. Blend with basil until smooth, then stir in cream if desired.

Creamy Celery Soup

Ingredients:

- 4 cups celery, chopped
- 1 onion, diced
- 4 cups vegetable broth
- 1 cup heavy cream (optional)
- Salt and pepper to taste

Instructions:

1. In a pot, sauté onion until soft.
2. Add celery and broth; bring to a boil.
3. Simmer until celery is tender, about 15-20 minutes.
4. Blend until smooth, then stir in cream if desired.

Tomato and Basil Bisque

Ingredients:

- 2 cans (14 oz each) crushed tomatoes
- 1 onion, diced
- 2 cloves garlic, minced
- 4 cups vegetable broth
- 1/2 cup fresh basil leaves
- 1 cup heavy cream (optional)
- Salt and pepper to taste

Instructions:

1. In a pot, sauté onion and garlic until soft.
2. Add crushed tomatoes, broth, salt, and pepper; bring to a boil.
3. Simmer for 15-20 minutes, then blend with basil until smooth.
4. Stir in cream if desired before serving.

Enjoy these delicious and comforting soups!

Chicken and Corn Chowder

Ingredients:

- 2 cups cooked chicken, shredded
- 4 cups corn (fresh or frozen)
- 1 onion, diced
- 2 potatoes, diced
- 4 cups chicken broth
- 1 cup heavy cream
- Salt and pepper to taste
- Chopped green onions for garnish

Instructions:

1. In a pot, sauté onion until soft.
2. Add potatoes, corn, and chicken broth; bring to a boil.
3. Reduce heat and simmer until potatoes are tender, about 15 minutes.
4. Stir in shredded chicken and cream; season with salt and pepper. Serve garnished with green onions.

Carrot and Ginger Soup

Ingredients:

- 1 pound carrots, chopped
- 1 onion, diced
- 1 tablespoon ginger, minced
- 4 cups vegetable broth
- 1 cup coconut milk
- Salt and pepper to taste

Instructions:

1. In a pot, sauté onion and ginger until softened.
2. Add carrots and broth; bring to a boil.
3. Simmer until carrots are tender, about 20 minutes.
4. Blend until smooth, stir in coconut milk, and season with salt and pepper.

Borscht (Beet Soup)

Ingredients:

- 3 medium beets, peeled and grated
- 1 onion, diced
- 2 carrots, diced
- 4 cups vegetable broth
- 1 tablespoon vinegar
- Salt and pepper to taste
- Sour cream and dill for serving

Instructions:

1. In a pot, sauté onion and carrots until soft.
2. Add beets, broth, vinegar, salt, and pepper; bring to a boil.
3. Reduce heat and simmer for about 30 minutes.
4. Serve hot, garnished with sour cream and dill.

Cheesy Cauliflower Chowder

Ingredients:

- 1 head cauliflower, chopped
- 1 onion, diced
- 4 cups vegetable broth
- 1 cup cheddar cheese, shredded
- 1 cup heavy cream
- Salt and pepper to taste

Instructions:

1. In a pot, sauté onion until soft.
2. Add cauliflower and broth; bring to a boil.
3. Simmer until cauliflower is tender, about 15 minutes.
4. Blend until smooth, then stir in cheese and cream until melted. Season with salt and pepper.

Southwestern Chicken Soup

Ingredients:

- 2 cups cooked chicken, shredded
- 1 can (15 oz) black beans, rinsed
- 1 can (14 oz) diced tomatoes
- 1 cup corn (fresh or frozen)
- 4 cups chicken broth
- 1 tablespoon chili powder
- Salt and pepper to taste

Instructions:

1. In a pot, combine chicken, beans, tomatoes, corn, broth, chili powder, salt, and pepper.
2. Bring to a boil, then reduce heat and simmer for 20 minutes.

Farro and Vegetable Soup

Ingredients:

- 1 cup farro, rinsed
- 1 onion, diced
- 2 carrots, diced
- 2 celery stalks, diced
- 4 cups vegetable broth
- 1 can (14 oz) diced tomatoes
- Salt and pepper to taste

Instructions:

1. In a pot, sauté onion, carrots, and celery until soft.
2. Add farro, broth, tomatoes, salt, and pepper; bring to a boil.
3. Reduce heat and simmer for about 30 minutes until farro is tender.

Lentil and Ham Soup

Ingredients:

- 1 cup lentils, rinsed
- 1 onion, diced
- 2 carrots, diced
- 2 celery stalks, diced
- 4 cups vegetable or chicken broth
- 1 cup diced ham
- Salt and pepper to taste

Instructions:

1. In a pot, sauté onion, carrots, and celery until softened.
2. Add lentils, broth, ham, salt, and pepper; bring to a boil.
3. Reduce heat and simmer for about 30-35 minutes until lentils are tender.

Miso Soup with Tofu

Ingredients:

- 4 cups dashi or vegetable broth
- 1/4 cup miso paste
- 1 cup tofu, cubed
- 1 cup sliced green onions
- 1 sheet nori, cut into strips (optional)

Instructions:

1. In a pot, heat dashi or broth until hot but not boiling.
2. In a bowl, mix miso paste with a little hot broth to dissolve.
3. Stir miso mixture back into the pot and add tofu and green onions.
4. Heat through and serve, garnished with nori if desired.

Enjoy these flavorful soups!

Curry Lentil Soup

Ingredients:

- 1 cup lentils, rinsed
- 1 onion, diced
- 2 carrots, diced
- 2 cloves garlic, minced
- 1 tablespoon curry powder
- 4 cups vegetable broth
- 1 can (14 oz) coconut milk
- Salt and pepper to taste
- Fresh cilantro for garnish

Instructions:

1. In a pot, sauté onion, carrots, and garlic until softened.
2. Add curry powder and cook for 1 minute until fragrant.
3. Stir in lentils and broth; bring to a boil.
4. Reduce heat and simmer until lentils are tender, about 25-30 minutes.
5. Stir in coconut milk, season with salt and pepper, and garnish with cilantro before serving.

Creamy Seafood Chowder

Ingredients:

- 1 pound mixed seafood (shrimp, scallops, fish)
- 1 onion, diced
- 2 potatoes, diced
- 4 cups seafood or fish stock
- 1 cup heavy cream
- 2 cloves garlic, minced
- Salt and pepper to taste
- Fresh parsley for garnish

Instructions:

1. In a pot, sauté onion and garlic until soft.
2. Add potatoes and stock; bring to a boil.
3. Reduce heat and simmer until potatoes are tender, about 15 minutes.
4. Stir in seafood and cook until just cooked through, about 5 minutes.
5. Add cream, season with salt and pepper, and garnish with parsley before serving.

Enjoy these delicious and comforting soups!

www.ingramcontent.com/pod-product-compliance
Lightning Source LLC
LaVergne TN
LVHW061956070526
838199LV00060B/4158